Dan Co...

By D.M. Longo

Illustrated by Tony Sansevero

Target Skill Consonants Dd/d/ and Kk/k/

Scott Foresman
is an imprint of

PEARSON

Can Dan see it?

Dan, look at it!

Can Dan hit it?

Look! Dan did it!

Can Dan see Kip?

Look at Kip, Dan!

See! Dan did it!